IT'S OK TO SAY NO
A BUCKET SYSTEM FOR LIVING

Valerie J Friesen

TRAFFORD
PUBLISHING

Note for Librarians: A cataloguing record for this book is available from Library and Archives Canada at www.collectionscanada.ca/amicus/index-e.html
ISBN 1-4120-9018-0

Printed in Victoria, BC, Canada. Printed on paper with minimum 30% recycled fibre.
Trafford's print shop runs on "green energy" from solar, wind and other environmentally-friendly power sources.

TRAFFORD
PUBLISHING™
Offices in Canada, USA, Ireland and UK

Book sales for North America and international:
Trafford Publishing, 6E–2333 Government St.,
Victoria, BC V8T 4P4 CANADA
phone 250 383 6864 (toll-free 1 888 232 4444)
fax 250 383 6804; email to orders@trafford.com
Book sales in Europe:
Trafford Publishing (UK) Limited, 9 Park End Street, 2nd Floor
Oxford, UK OX1 1HH UNITED KINGDOM
phone +44 (0)1865 722 113 (local rate 0845 230 9601)
facsimile +44 (0)1865 722 868; info.uk@trafford.com
Order online at:
trafford.com/06-0774

10 9 8 7 6 5 4

About the Author

Valerie J. Friesen

Valerie J. Friesen (Val) is an upbeat, friendly, caring and "easy to talk to" gal. She started a Counselling Service in order to meet the growing needs of people who struggle with life's challenges.

A Masters Degree in Counselling and Life Coaching training plus a "heart" for people is her unique fomula for helping over four thousand individuals, couples and families in the seventeen years she has been serving the community.

Val's desire was to help people in a meaningful way and this remains her strong focus today.

In Val's spare time she enjoys golfing, travel, camping, friends, photography, kayaking, walking, gardening and music. Balance in her life and with her time has proven to be an important factor in her success and longevity as a Counsellor.

As you read through It's OK To Say NO, Val's second book, you will discover that she is a person of integrity and a person you can count on to provide top notch, practical and "to the point" information to help you along your journey. She provides top notch Counselling and Personal Improvement Coaching Services.

TABLE OF CONTENTS

Stop being a chameleon.
Stop struggling emotionally.
Live with integrity.
Thinking affects your feelings.

INTRODUCTION

Who could benefit from reading a book like this?

Every adult could benefit from reading a book like this.

This bucket system for living is designed for the adult who is not able to say no to people and challenges that come their way in life. They do not say no, neither do they know when to say no.

Maybe you will identify with one of the following types of people.

Do you take good care of yourself and do you make good choices for you?

Do you say yes to requests, even though it is not a good choice for you?

Do you have a tough time making decisions? Or, defer decisions to someone else?

Do you operate in life by "winging it"? Or by "flying by the seat of your pants"?

Do you lack direction and purpose?

Did you have a difficult childhood and are you still being affected by it?

Have you been in an unhealthy relationship for years and feel like there is nothing of you left? Maybe you need some healing.

Did something happen to you around the years of your late teens and early twenties, which caused you to not develop your identity? Examples of life events which may have side tracked you could include a car accident or physical injury, sexual abuse, a loss of a friend or family member by death, addiction to drugs or alcohol, depression and poor self esteem.

Do you know how to think well and communicate to others what is important to you and what you believe?

Do you take things personally?

Do you worry what others think?

Do you struggle emotionally?

Then this bucket system is for you.

Every teenager could benefit from reading this book too. Developing our identity occurs in our late teen years and early twenties. This information on a bucket system for living would make these transition years much smoother.

The purpose of *It's OK To Say No – A Bucket System For Living* is to help you develop a system for living that you can use everyday, to help you make good choices for yourself. Once you have developed your system, you can use it for years to come; helping you to make good choices, to see clearly what is good for you and what is not and most importantly, to say no to what is not good for you and yes to what is good for you.

The benefits of having your own personal bucket system is that you will not struggle emotionally as much, you will think better, you will not take things personally, nor worry what others think. You will begin to think of your self differently and your self-esteem will grow and flourish.

For those readers who feel lost and maybe feel broken from experiencing significant trauma or damage in their lives, then this bucket system will assist you in rebuilding and healing. Imagine the wonderful gift of feeling whole once more. Once you have your bucket system for living, it will be easier to see who you are and to feel good about yourself again. To help one person to experience wholeness again, this book would be worth it.

Finally, maybe you are the reader that never established your own identity and have been winging it through life. With your bucket system for living you can begin to live a meaningful and purposeful life; life won't just be something that happens to you, life will become what you make it become for yourself.

Give this book a try. You will be glad you did.

CHAPTER I
THE BASICS

Why a bucket?

The principles that are going to be discussed are so abstract that it is sometimes hard to understand them. A bucket makes it simple. We are going to bring together all the things that form who we are and collect them in a bucket. The bucket becomes a visual tool to see what we are bringing together and forming.

A bucket is a container to collect all of those things that make us a "somebody," and so the bucket is a very functional tool. You can visualize that you place one item after another into the bucket, eventually filling it up to the top.

Therefore, the bucket concept takes the abstract concept of identity and makes it concrete. It makes it visual and also provides a container to put "who we are" into, and it becomes a helpful tool. You can easily visualize a bucket. Imagine a bucket that is galvanized metal or a bright red plastic one.

11

One person I met used a basket and brought together all the things that made her who she was, placing them into her basket. I can imagine small eggs or a collection of seashells or small pebbles. Can you see a large basket with a long handle wrapped around her arm? One boyfriend asked his girlfriend how her pail was. She looked back at him quizzically and tried to figure out what he was asking. Then it occurred to her. He was asking her about her bucket and they laughed as they realized the irony of their terminology.

Another alternative to a bucket could be a knap-sack. A woman I met filled her knapsack with all the things that made her "a somebody". A closer option to a bucket would be a box. I recommend a bucket and this idea will become clearer as you read along.

The total picture of what I am talking about is just beginning to take shape. Hang in there and read on.

WHAT GOES IN YOUR BUCKET?

1. Characteristics

There are basically four things that you put into your bucket. The first are your characteristics. Imagine making a list of characteristics that describe who you are as a person. A characteristic is an adjective or a describing word of who you are, for example, nice, kind, friendly and honest. Take a moment to jot down a list of characteristics describing yourself. Just get started. You can come back to the list again and again to revise it.

A list something like this: Your list

kind   _____
friendly   _____
out going   _____
honest   _____
goofy   _____
calm   _____

2. Roles

The second item that belongs in your bucket is your roles. The primary roles that we have are "worker", "friend", "spouse" and "parent". Secondary roles include "brother" or "sister", and "son" or "daughter".

Quickly jot down the role of worker and begin describing the kind of worker you are. Use adjectives to make it simple. For example, you may be an organized, reliable, fun, punctual and thorough worker.

You will want to describe the type of worker you are currently and you may want to include the type of worker you want to be. For instance, you may not be totally punctual, but you want to strive to be more. Put this under worker and begin being the person you want to be.

A list something like this:	Your list:
Worker	Worker
responsible	_____
hard working	_____
fun	_____
punctual	_____

Now, you may not be a spouse or parent yet. I would recommend that you jot down these roles and begin picturing what you would be like in each of these roles. It's okay to plan ahead and predetermine what kind of spouse and parent you think you want to be. In fact, this is ideal – to plan ahead and decide for yourself who you are going to be.

A list something like this:	Your list:
Spouse	Spouse
friend	_____
loving	_____
fun	_____
faithful	_____

As you begin working through these little exercises one question you might have is – "am I writing down who I am now? Or who I want to be?" The answer would be both. Gradually you are forming the person you want to be by making small choices that will add together to form the whole.

To further clarify what a role is and how you would define yours, let us explore the role of friend. What kind of friend are you? What kind of friend would you like to be?

A list something like this:	Your list:
Friend	Friend
fun	_____
available	_____
supportive	_____
listener	_____

There are a variety of types of friends we have but the core role in terms of who we are comes from our own definition. Begin to figure out what kind of friend you want to be and then begin being it.

Put everything we are working on together on a worksheet. It may look something like this:

Characteristics	Roles

<u>Characteristics</u>

kind
friendly
out going
honest
goofy
calm

<u>Roles</u>

<u>worker</u>
responsible
hard working
fun
punctual

<u>spouse</u>
friend
loving
fun
faithful

<u>friend</u>
fun
available
supportive
listener

<u>parent</u>

<u>daughter/son</u>

3. Values

The third item that is included in an individuals bucket is values. Values are statements that describe what is important to us. Start your value statements with **It is important to me...** and then begin to complete the sentence.

It is important to me to trust others.
It is important to me to be dressed for the occasion.
It is important to me to be respected.
It is important to me to pay my bills on time.
It is important to me to have things that I am excited about.
It is important to me to have a hobby.
It is important to me not to drink alcohol.
It is important to me not to smoke.

Imagine the possibilities of the values you may have! Most of you will have lots of values already formed and will find it a challenge to figure them out and write them down on paper. Get started today and then revisit this exercise several times until you think your list is complete.

Your list:

It is important to me...

1.

2.

3.

4.

5.

6.

7.

8.

The values that you will want to identify in this section are ones that remain the same year after year. From our core values we make the many daily choices in our lives. For example, after explaining the bucket to my sister, she asked if it would be correct to have "It is important to me to do knitting." I reassured her that it was OK to have this in her list of values yet it might be better to have "It is important to me to have a hobby". This year she chooses knitting and when she changes to crocheting or quilt making, indicating that her value "it is important to me to have a hobby," remains the same and only her choice has changed. Another example of a core value could be "It is important to me to exercise and to be physically active". Such a wise value and it provides a lifetime of options and opportunities. With a value like this you could choose to walk, play tennis, kayak, play golf, or do yoga. Actually you might want to do all of these or at different times in your life you choose one or the other. Maybe you play golf in the summer and ski in the winter. The value of exercising or being physically active remains the same.

A critical point of identifying values is that we choose the values that we want to place in our bucket and then they become our own. Yes! We own our values. This will be elaborated on later, but the jest is to say that some of our values come from adopting values from others or rejecting values of others.

It may be fashionable for your friends to drink or go to parties. It would be fine if you choose that you want to be alcohol free or be a sports person (rather than a party person). What you choose is what you choose. It is your value and you can own it. You do not have to feel bad about the value you have because you decided it was the right one for you.

Characteristics	Roles	Values.
kind	<u>worker</u>	**It is important to me…**
friendly	responsible	- to trust others
out going	hard working	- to be dressed for the
honest	fun	occasion
goofy	punctual	- to be respected
calm		- to pay my bills on time
	<u>spouse</u>	- to have things I am
	friend	excited about
	loving	- to have a hobby
	fun	- not to drink alcohol
	faithful	- not to smoke
	<u>friend</u>	
	fun	
	available	
	supportive	
	listener	
	<u>parent</u>	
	<u>daughter/son</u>	

4. Beliefs

The fourth and final item that goes into a bucket is your beliefs. Beliefs are very similar to values but are worded slightly differently. They are more like statements. The best way to describe a belief is to give you some examples.

I am an OK person.
It is OK to speak up.
It is OK to make decisions for myself.
It is OK to have an opinion.
God loves me.
Not everyone has to like me.

To elaborate on the last example, I struggled for years with needing people to like me. I thought this was something to believe. When I changed my belief to "not everyone has to like me," then I felt so much better and wasn't bothered so much when people didn't like me.

Remember you already have many beliefs that you live by and that you are just starting to think about them as being beliefs. You are putting the beliefs into words and jotting them down. What you want to do is write down the beliefs about things you have already discovered and then write down some beliefs that you would like to include in your way of living. Place these new beliefs in your bucket.

For example,

I am capable.

A man I once encountered said that he often felt and thought that he was not capable of doing things. His belief was "I am not capable". As he looked closer at his bucket he began to realize that he could make a choice and that he no longer had to live by this self-defeating belief. He built a new belief, opposite to his old belief, which is "I am capable" and placed this into his new bucket.

I am a good person.

A 44 year old woman always had been told that "I am not a good person" from a variety of life experiences. She began to explore the possibility that she no longer had to believe this and she could choose to believe "I am a good person". This was a dynamic change in her thinking and brought about many positive new feelings and changes in her behavior.

Essentially she needed to believe that "I am an OK person". To think anything less creates inferiority and insecurity.

It is OK to make a mistake.

All the perfectionists reading this need to take a breath and let this sink in. It would be a radical change for some of you who are professed perfectionists who firmly believe "I can never make a mistake" to change it to "It is OK to make a mistake". Yes, this new thinking is radical but certainly rewarding and absolutely life changing. Take it a step further and reinforce your new belief with the value "It is important to me to do my best". In no time at all you would start to relax and not be near as hard on yourself. Things in life would come to you much easier and with less effort. Celebrate your accomplishments and relish the feelings of completion and accomplishment - abolishing the empty feelings of failing and constantly falling short.

Together we have studied and identified the basics of the contents of your bucket. The four basic ingredients are your characteristics, roles, values and beliefs. Your work sheet may start to look like this example.

Characteristics	Roles	Values.
kind		**It is important to me...**
friendly	worker	- to trust others
out going	responsible	- to be dressed for the
honest	hard working	occasion
goofy	fun	- to be respected
calm	punctual	- to pay my bills on time
		- to have things I am
	spouse	excited about
	friend	- to have a hobby
	loving	- not to drink alcohol
	fun	- not to smoke
	faithful	
		Beliefs
		I am an OK person
	friend	It is OK to speak up
	fun	It is OK to make decisions
	available	for myself
	supportive	It is OK to have an opinion
	listener	God loves me
		Not everyone has to
		like me
	parent	
	daughter/son	

INDIVIDUATION

Individuation is a concept that refers to the necessity of deciding for ourselves who we are and we do this by borrowing from others traits or values and adopting them as our own. For example, I met a woman who just would not be swayed to be critical. She was reluctant to give opinion or knock anyone else down. She spoke only in terms of positive support. This positive nature I placed in my bucket.

Another woman I met was a "lover of life." She enjoyed life to the fullest and this is also something I put in my bucket. My college room mate enjoyed the small things in life and from her I learned that I also could enjoy the small things in life.

While we adopt for ourselves traits or values to place in our bucket, there is also the necessity to throw some things out and formulate our own value. For example, back to the dreaded punctuality illustration. My situation was a little different because I was raised that we go to events early and be ready for the activity. My parents often went to the airport early in the event we had a flat tire or the traffic was backed up. They covered every thing that might happen. I can recall as a teenager going to a choir practice or youth activity early and then having to wait for everyone to arrive. i would become frustrated and irritated at the fashionable late people. To top it off we would never start on time. The value would be worded like this, "It is important to me to be on time". I kept the punctuality but decided that for me it would be better to be just on time.

Choices, Bits and Pieces.

Building and establishing an identity is not typically done in one large chunk, rather it occurs over time with conscious effort. A bucket is filled by making small choices that together to form an identity. These small choices are referred to as "bits and pieces."

CUPS

There is one more "basic" that you should know about and that is the concept of the "cup". A cup is adding to our metaphor of the bucket and it requires you to really use your imagination. Imagine that a cup can scoop up each and every piece that you put into your bucket. This means that each characteristic, role, value or belief is like something that can be scooped up with a cup.

Go ahead, draw a cup on your page. Place your cup beside your bucket.

CHAPTER II
COMMONLY ASKED QUESTIONS

1. The content of this bucket you are suggesting is quite different than what society says determines who we are. What should I believe?

Yes, the concept society has of what forms our identity is dramatically different than what I am suggesting. Society's concept of what makes a person a somebody is definitely affected by peer pressure, culture and marketing. You will come across many others who have built their identity on something far different that what is being suggested in this book.

I have come across two people who said their identity was based on their good looks. The female was a model and the male was a fireman. Both had depended on their looks to define who they are and get them what they wanted in life. The male suggested he rides through life because of his good looks.

Others depend on their wealth to determine who they are. This may include the money they have or the money they are currently making. Essentially they have "I am wealthy" in their bucket.

For a couple of years in my early twenties I placed my little 1978 MGB Convertible Sports Car in my bucket. I was a "somebody" because I drove such a great looking car. To own and drive a small desirable sports car made me feel young and trendy.

Others have bought in to the idea that they have identity because of what family they are from or because of some unique identifying role, such as political leader, CEO of a company, or top sales person in the company.

If you start thinking about these bucket contents, you might begin to see that any of these could be taken away or lost. You can have a sports car or have a prestigious position in the company or have good looks <u>but</u> tomorrow they could be gone. I call these **pseudo** identities.

2. This bucket idea sounds so selfish, is it? (the question asked most often).

It is a stretch for many of us to consider taking care of ourselves before we take care of others. It seems absolutely selfish. Often we hear of the importance to help others and care for others but this becomes so extreme that it can make a person actually physically ill. Just so you know – it's OK to take care of self. In fact, it is imperative!

To put the answer to this question succinctly – the better we take care of self, the better we are at all of our roles. By putting yourself first, you become a better mother, spouse, friend and worker.

There is no doubt this thinking can be a foreign idea for you. Likely it is absolutely opposite to what you may have been taught. Females have been nurtured from very early on to serve and care for others. Our mothers modeled this behavior and taught us to be the same. Another source is for the Christian, who is encouraged Sunday after Sunday to serve and help others. If you are a mother, then you believe your children should come first, before everything else. If you are all three sources, mother, Christian and female, then I call this the *triple whammy*.

The principles suggested in this book are about taking care of self and these principles are neither selfish nor self-centered. It is the simple process that we all must go through in order to be all that we can be and to effectively carry out all the challenges life affords.

3. Val you mentioned the Christian. Where does God fit into all of this?

God and our faith in God fits nicely in with your bucket contents. The Bible is full of psychological ideas and much of psychology is derived from the scriptures. I would suggest that identity formation can include both God and the suggested contents of this book.

My experience when working on my bucket was to place into my belief section, four key beliefs found in scripture. I had heard these as a child in Sunday School.

I am a child of God.
God loves me.
God made me.
I am special.

When forming my identity I personally adopted these extremely profound little statements to form the very foundation of my bucket. I used these basic truths and personally chose to place them in the bottom inches of my total contents. Therefore, the heart of my bucket is these beliefs and then on these four beliefs I have placed all the other contents of who I am. So it can be for you.

What ever your spiritual belief system, the beliefs from your spirituality can be placed into your bucket. Incorporate them as part of who you are.

I am a child of God.
God loves me.
God made me.
I am special.

CHAPTER III
STRENGTHENING AREAS IN YOUR LIFE

BUILDING YOUR SELF-ESTEEM

One excellent use of the bucket is to establish a healthy self-esteem. The basic premise is "how you think affects how you feel." What do you think about yourself? Maybe you think or know you are over weight, too short or extremely shy. You could think you are stupid or not capable. Because you are less than what you want to be, you do not <u>think</u> well of yourself and then you would not <u>feel</u> good about yourself.

In order to turn poor self-esteem around, you may need to change how you <u>think</u> about yourself. If you base how you think about yourself on your inadequacies then you will feel low-self esteem. If you base how you think about yourself on your characteristics, roles, values and beliefs, then you will have a strong self-esteem.

how you think,
affects how you feel

You and I both need to look at what bothers us and try to realize that we are not perfect nor never will be. However, we are terrific individuals that have a full and complete bucket. Just because we are dissatisfied with a part of our life, our buckets can still be full and we are being the individuals we want to be. This full bucket – how you think about yourself- is the best way to build a strong self-esteem.

IMPROVING YOUR SELF-CONCEPT

The primary usage of the bucket is to build a healthy self-concept. A self-concept is a picture or a mental image of how we are. A self-concept is a way of thinking about our selves.

Once you go through the exercise of articulating your characteristics, roles, values and beliefs, the picture of you will become clear. All of the things that you may have used to picture yourself fall to the side and the real you will come to the surface.

GROWING YOUR CONFIDENCE

This third items fits nicely in place as a follow-up to self-concept (how you think about yourself) and self-esteem (how you feel about yourself). If you can clearly know who you are then you will start to feel good about yourself and from these you will begin to have confidence!

Confidence is how you behave. If you think and feel good about yourself, then you will begin to behave confidently.

Careful, others will notice!

Take a step back and build your bucket. From a full bucket you will begin to experience an entirely new level of confidence. Careful, others will notice!

BECOMING MORE ASSERTIVE

If you want to become more assertive, the bucket can help you with this as well. The belief section of the bucket can hold assertive beliefs that can guide you in a variety of situations. For instance:

It is OK to speak up.
It is OK to say no.
It is OK to take care of yourself.
It is OK to stand up for yourself.

In a particular situation, when the emotions run high, you can go to your belief section of your bucket, where it might give some direction for you, such as, "It is OK to speak up." Instead of becoming flustered, you would speak up. This would be a totally different response than what you would normally have. The results would be more effective.

What the bucket does is provide "thinking" direction in the middle of an emotional situation. By thinking clearer you are better able to express yourself.

MAKING GOOD CHOICES

Similar to becoming more assertive, a person can also make better choices in life by "thinking" better. The bucket provides a person with a system to make choices. Either the option fits with all of your values and does not take a cup out, or it doesn't.

Small choices eventually add up to increasing happiness and personal life satisfaction. Happiness grows in bits and pieces. Choices help you establish and build the life you designed, so you can be the person you want to be.

APPLYING A PERSONAL RESOURCE SYSTEM

Every bucket will be unique as the person who filled the bucket. Once the bucket is filled, then you will have a way to think and a personal system to help you navigate life. The secret is to make decisions that follow the contents of your bucket and not to make decisions where a cup or maybe several cups may come out.

Keeping the cups in your bucket is the operative concept. Remember you can make a choice that takes a cup out or someone else can insist you do something that takes a cup out. By keeping the cups in your bucket you will live with a renewed inner satisfaction for life.

Recently, I was watching a television interview with Tiger Woods and his father, a former military man. When Tiger was a young man, his father would insist that Tiger think of a series of eight steps to use each time he addressed the golf ball. His father called these steps a SOP, which stands for standard operating procedure.

At first, Tiger would reluctantly think through each step before striking the ball. Eventually each step became automatic and almost effortless. Tiger's SOP is similar to a bucket. Your bucket can become your SOP and a resource system that you turn to each time you make a decision in life. At first it will require some work, but eventually it will become effortless.

Remember your bucket is your personalized system for living. It's yours and it's OK to enjoy it.

CREATING AND GENERATING GOOD FEELINGS

The more you use your bucket to make choices in life, the happier you will be. If you make a choice and no cup comes out of your bucket then you will get a good feeling. If you make a choice and a cup comes out of your bucket, then you will have a bad feeling. For example, if you want to be a patient person and you act impatiently, then a cup will come out. When you behave patiently then the cup will stay in. In this instance a cup is the characteristic "patient".

I heard about the story of a man who noticed he had a bad feeling and began to think about what is creating this bad feeling. He realized that he was being impatient. He had decided earlier that week to be more patient. Once he realized this, he changed his behavior and began to behave patiently. The bad feeling which made him feel uncomfortable went away and he began to feel calm and happy. He used the bad feeling as an indicator to let him know something was wrong.

I can imagine that if you don't have a bucket or a personal operating system, then the good and bad feelings would be so mixed. The idea is to generate as many good feelings as possible, in fact flood your life with good feelings and live a "10" on the happiness scale.

If you had a scale of 1 to 10, how happy are you? If "10" indicates happy and 1 is unhappy, what number would you designate to the general level of happiness? For example, you might be a 3 or a 6 or best yet an 8.

Then begin to plan out what it would take to move to a 9.5 on the happiness scale. What would you need to change to move up one number and maybe two or three numbers?

The bottom line is to realize that there is a direct correlation between living with your bucket and happiness. By following your values and beliefs and by being the person that your characteristics say you are, then your happiness will go up and up.

MOVING IN A MEANINGFUL DIRECTION

Have you ever felt like you are winging it or that you are flying by the seat of your pants? You may be making a series of choices that together do not make a bit of sense nor are they connected in any way. Maybe you are unfocused and are randomly doing things that make it feel like you are "winging it." It may be that you do not have a bucket. It could be that you have met someone else who comes across as "flying by the seat of their pants".

On the other hand, maybe you are winging it and flying by the seat of your pants. Are you? If either is true, one answer is to establish a bucket. Making choices from central source – your bucket, will help to make positive, healthy choices that connect together in a meaningful way.

You make choices every day, maybe several every hour that together can impact your life. Remember the small choices add up. By making the choices based on a clearly established identity, you can know that either a choice fits your bucket or it does not. By keeping the cups in your bucket and consistently making choices that fit with the kind of person you are, then you <u>will</u> <u>not</u> <u>be</u> winging it. By allowing the cups to come out from your bucket and making choices that only sometimes fit with the kind of person you are, then you <u>will</u> <u>be</u> winging it.

Imagine how much less stress you would have by "not" winging it! Imagine how much happier you would be. Imagine how choice after choice would fit together and help you establish a consistent meaningful life.

STOP WORRYING ABOUT
WHAT PEOPLE THINK

Probably all of us worry about what people think to some degree. There are some people who are so preoccupied with this type of worry that they never experience the freedom to be them selves. Would it not be a wonderful thing not to be preoccupied with what people think?

I had just come out of a restaurant and my good friend commented to me, "you are so cheap." She was making reference to the fact that in our luncheon that day the price of my lunch was under two dollars. Her comment caught me off guard and I was stunned. Nonetheless, I was deeply hurt and I began to struggle emotionally.

**Experience the freedom
to be yourself.**

Typically a situation like this would bother me for days, but it was different this time. The first thing I did was look to my bucket for I knew it would help me sort this out. I looked at my characteristic list and did not see the characteristic cheap or anything like it on the list. I searched through my values and came up empty. Then I began to think about the type of person I was decided an appropriate characteristic was generous which was not even remotely close to being "cheap."

Yes, I decided that I was a generous person. I know I pay my part of bills and often pitch in to help pay the part of the bill for others. I am far from cheap, more so I am actually responsible and leaning toward generous. My emotions started to calm down and I could begin to think clearer. I knew I was not cheap and that she said a very hurtful comment.

Now that I was thinking clearer I started to become more objective and less subjective. I began to realize that she did not know the entire story. She was not aware that I was not feeling well that day and that I actually should have stayed home in bed because of my flue like feeling. Venturing out to go for lunch with a group of friends became my priority and I decided to go but have very little to eat. I had looked forward to attending this luncheon for a long time. I did not want to miss out.

However, my friend did not know this information and must have concluded since I contributed so little to the bill that I must be cheap.

I continued to recover from this excruciating blow of being called "cheap."

More objective thoughts crossed my mind. I

started to realize that her comment was simply inappropriate and she had basically attacked me by saying "You". "You are so cheap." Of course I should have been stunned. My emotions were appropriate for the blow I had experienced.

Furthermore I began to realize that this friend who had hurt me so bad this day was the same person I leant money to a few years earlier for a dress she needed for graduation. I was not cheap then and I am not cheap now. She just did not think before she spoke, nor did she have enough information.

Typically I would have struggled emotionally for several days. This time I was able to recuperate, within a few short hours, by using my bucket. I knew clearly how to think and I decided not to worry about what she thought.

Many times in our lives another person will say something that will be very hurtful and we will worry about what they think. Our bucket provides a mainstay of information that will help us out in the crunch.

STOP TAKING THINGS PERSONALLY

Similarly to not worrying about what people think, a bucket can help you not to be such a sensitive person. Often we take things personally and suffer needlessly. Are you over sensitive?

To be able to think objectively certainly helps. In my bucket I placed two crucial values that have helped me so much. One is to stay away from people who knock me down and the second is to hang out with people who build me up. For years I believed it was vital to have everyone like me and I would put up with people who were negative and knocked me down emotionally. Once I had these two values guiding which people I kept company with, I had much better results emotionally.

Why struggle so much with people who put you down all the time. Stay away from them and gravitate toward those who nourish and help you to bloom.

In my belief system I placed another helpful belief. The belief was "not everyone has to like me." This was a giant new way to think. I would use this belief time and time to deal with people and difficult situations and it would help me to let things roll off my back and be less sensitive.

The reality is that not everyone gets along. Even good friends do not always get along. Each day is not always perfect. As you relax and take things in stride, then you will begin to not take things so personally.

At a conference banquet I quickly took my assigned seat because my feet were so sore. I sat at my table all alone. Then I gazed over to the other side of the room and saw people who were also waiting were looking at me. My mind flashed several thoughts – they must think I am alone, that I am weird and that no one likes me. I panicked sitting there by myself.

I knew I needed to start thinking objectively. My bucket reminded me that I was easy to talk to and friendly. I also knew I was kind and that I had good friends. My panic began to subside. I began to think more rationally for after all, I was alone simply because my friends had just gone to the washroom first. I beat them to the table. I was totally OK sitting there and that friends who accompanied me that day would be coming along. Soon, I felt better.

The minutes passed while I sat at the table by myself. I started to enjoy a few minutes of solitude and stopped being preoccupied with what I thought they were thinking across the room. I felt at peace and very comfortable. My emotional struggle was over. The emotional outcome was very different once I had changed my thinking from being preoccupied with what others might be thinking to the fact I was totally OK.

BEING ABLE TO SAY NO

How many things do you do in a day or in the week that you do not really want to do? How well do you think you take care of self? Are you feeling like you are spinning your wheels doing numerous things and think you are getting no where? Do you do things that are not good for you to be doing?

You may need a bucket.

Quick. Do it quick. Place "it's OK to say no." in your bucket before anyone sees you. Go ahead. It goes in your belief section.

It may seem awkward and uncomfortable to have such a foreign belief in your bucket, but it is one of the more healthy things you can do for yourself.

When you are struggling with too many things to do or you find yourself doing things that you do not enjoy you can go to your bucket and find the answer. It is OK to say no.

Your bucket now holds a belief that will guide your choices for the rest of your life. It is a pivotal belief that will steer you towards doing things and making choices that are meaningful, away from choices that seem to get you no where.

Starting out with this new belief might take a little time getting used to. I remember the early days with this new belief. I can recall being asked to do something and three days later calling back and replying that I will not be able to help out. I usually came up with a great excuse.

Gradually I was able to say no sooner. I would call back in two days, then a day later and then several hours. Each time I experienced this elation that I had said no and patted myself on the back. I was extremely proud of my new skill.

Eventually I was able to say no when I was asked and never felt compelled to provide a reason. Saying no did not mean I never volunteered again, it meant that I would no longer be volunteering for everything that came along and that what I did choose to do would be more meaningful and satisfying. My happiness began to increase.

Do you ever feel like you have to have an excuse for why you are saying no? I used to think this and then I figured this out in a fresh new way. I was received a telephone call asking me to subscribe to the newspaper and I expressed that I was not interested. The caller began to explain that they were providing two weeks free for me to try out their newspaper. I quickly replied that I was not really interested.

The caller was bewildered and asked why I would not take a free newspaper for two weeks. He explained it was free and that there were no strings attached. I simply was not interested and indicated that I had no reason. I never thought I needed to provide a reason either. I simply did not want the newspaper.

It is OK to say no and we do not have to provide a reason. In some cases it would be fine to explain why you are not able to come or why you do not want to participate, but a reason is not always necessary. It is OK just to say a polite no.

Two senior women were discussing that they had both been asked to help out with something at their church. Chuckling together one told the other that she said "no" and it felt good. People of all ages are learning this valuable lesson that it is OK to say no.

A way to make more time at work is to be able to say no to coworkers or no to assignments that are asked of you. One woman I met said that she did not mind helping other coworkers but it distracted her from her task. The next time she was asked a question her new response was "I would love to help you but I am going to finish the task I am on now. Could we look at your problem in ten minutes?"

ACHIEVING BALANCE IN YOUR LIFE

How can I establish and maintain balance in my life? Some would say this is a million dollar question and if you figure out the answer you will make a million dollars. Yes, to achieve balance in your life is not easy especially with all the demands and challenges life brings our way.

As you have been reading we have been learning that saying "no" is vital to establishing and maintaining a healthy balance in your life. For example, if you are a spouse and a friend – remember the different roles you have. Your friend asks you to come over and help work on his fence that he is fixing up. At the same time you had a previous commitment to go with your spouse to pick out light fixtures. When you say no to your friend you are no less a friend, and you continue being the spouse you want to be.

Furthermore, examine your characteristics list, and make a mental note that by going with your spouse to the lighting store you remain helpful, caring and considerate. All these characteristics stay in tact and no cups come out.

There may be a couple ways of looking at the choice you have to make – should I go to the lighting store with my spouse or should I help my friend with their fence? Remember the secret to making a good sound choice is not to let any cups come out of your bucket.

You may want to say to your friend that you will help them with their fence later but you want to go to the lighting store first. This way you keep the balance between spouse and friend. Remember that saying no can be done politely and tactfully.

Another good example is the worker role. Work takes the majority of our time and effort in the day and yet we have other roles to fulfill. They might include parent, son/daughter, and spouse. Oh yes, there also needs to be time for self, including a good rest. How can you achieve a balance?

Sometimes family or friends encroach on being

the worker we want and need to be. Family life can be demanding and you might not be focused at work or even over tired. Getting adequate sleep is vital to being the worker you want and need to be.

In short - attempt to figure out what really is most important to you and then begin focusing your time and energy in this direction. Politely say no to things that do not fit. Do not do any one thing in excess. Keep all of your roles and values in mind when you are making choices. Finally, remember it is OK to take care of you.

STOP BEING A CHAMELEON

There are many people who go through most of their life behaving like a chameleon. A chameleon is a small lizard like animal that is able to change their appearance by changing their skin color, in order to fit into their surroundings. People who are chameleons do not have a bucket or a clear sense of identity they become whatever anyone else wants them to become. Essentially they change their color to suit the situation and to suit others.

People who do not have buckets are like chameleons. They can also be described as individuals who "wing it" or go through life "by the seat of their pants."

Have you ever met an individual like this? I have. Recently I met a neighbor who was exactly a chameleon. I began telling her several things about myself as we got acquainted and she began to tell me how she was involved in some of the same activities as me. She was doing a fantastic job of building bridges of friendship.

Through the months I have watched her and what she told me that day and what she actually does is quite the contrary. It is apparent that she is not the person she proclaimed to be. She was a chameleon. When we first met she adapted to what I was saying and claimed to be the same. She will be whatever the other person wants her to be and says things to fit in. Likely she has a great need to be accepted.

Can you tell the difference between individuals who have a bucket/identity and those who do not?

If you are not able to tell the difference yet, this will change and you will be able to differentiate, as you look closer at the people you meet.

STOP STRUGGLING EMOTIONALLY

Part of navigating a healthy relationship is to be constantly declaring your values and beliefs. Remembering this point helps you rebound from tough situations much easier and far more quickly. If you are expressing an opinion and you are put down for it, then simply declare your belief, "it's okay to have an opinion." If someone speaks unkindly to you, declare your value, "please speak nicely." If a person pressures you into doing something you do not want to do, declare your belief, "it's okay to do what I right and good for me." If a person insists on having your help, declare your value, "it's okay to say no."

**Living from the
Inside Out.**

LIVE WITH INTEGRITY

A contemporary phrase that is soon replacing the word integrity is *living from the inside out.* They both mean roughly the same thing, which involves knowing who we are and what is important to us and then live by our own system. Rather than living by what other people want, we live by what is inside of us. Thus, we live from the inside out.

Believing one thing and doing another is not integrity. Believing one thing and living it out in our life is integrity.

Seniors in particular struggle to find integrity as they look back over the years. They look back and reminisce about their lives in order to feel good about the choices they made and the things they did. When they

CHAPTER IV
THE BUCKET SYSTEM FOR RELATIONSHIPS

HOW DOES A RELATIONSHIP WORK WHEN BOTH PEOPLE HAVE A BUCKET?

The bucket presents us with a wonderful tool to navigate relationships. To begin, each person in the relationship must first build their bucket and know the contents of the bucket thoroughly. Once both individuals have a bucket the navigation of the relationship can begin.

The focal point of any healthy relationship is that both parties can be themselves. Each person can make good choices and take good care of self. Essentially, a healthy relationship begins with two healthy people.

A healthy relationship begins with two healthy people.

Navigating the relationship requires good negotiation, where the couple make decisions together that do not compromise any bucket contents. Often relationships require compromising. This becomes a tricky area to work with. Yes, there is a place for compromise but the compromise cannot involve taking a cup out of your or their bucket.

Go ahead and compromise on issues that do not cost you anything. At the same time hold tight to your values and characteristics.

For instance, you may be a person who does not want to drink alcohol or party where alcohol is involved. Your spouse or the person you are dating may drink regularly and want to party all the time. The values are obviously incompatible.

Another example is where one person wants to be a trusting person and the other person thinks it is OK to lie. It would be very difficult for the first person to be trusting because the second person does not behave in a trustworthy manner.

Examples are important, let me provide you with a few more. The most important value a person has in their bucket is that "It is important to be respected." This makes it imperative that the second person respects the first in their behavior or how they speak. I have come across couples where neither are respectful of the other and cups are flying out of their buckets.

To insist on being respected would be a basic value for most people who are healthy individuals.

In my bucket I have the value "it is important to hang out with people who build me up." Plus, "it is important to stay away from people who knock me down." My tendency is to gravitate to those people who are encouraging and have positive things to say and stay away from those who a negative and put me down. When a relationship is mutually encouraging and equal then the relationship can be healthy.

Often two people can have distinct differences in how they think money should be managed. One couple I came across had similar values and characteristics in all areas except their values about money. One spouse wanted to take risks and invest money while the other valued having a nest egg and some buffer to fall back on when needed. It would be very difficult to navigate healthy relationship with these two people. The solution would be for both to be able to maintain their values. Neither should compromise.

It is easy to detest another person who thinks different and put them down for what they think. Rather our attitude should be one of respect for the other and acceptance of what they believe.

WHY DO I KEEP PICKING THE WRONG TYPE OF WOMEN? OR MEN?

Individuals who do not know who they are and do

not have an identity do not have a system to guide them in their relationship choices. It is essential to clearly know who you are, including knowing your values and beliefs. Once you have established a clear identity, then you also want to meet a man or woman, someone who you are considering as a future partner, who has a bucket as well.

How many times have you tried to have a relationship with someone who does not have an identity? Are you trying to have a relationship with someone else who is totally lost and is going through life winging it? This may be a large part of why you are picking the wrong person.

The other aspect is that you need to know who you are and what is important to you. How many times have you tried to have a relationship when you yourself have been floundering and struggling along? Are you trying to have a relationship with someone when you yourself are totally lost and going through life winging it?

There are two essential ingredients when finding the "right person" for you. First, the right type of person for you is an individual who knows who <u>they</u> are and you can clearly see who <u>they</u> are. Secondly, the right type of person for you is one who sees who <u>you</u> are and lets you be <u>you</u>.

The closer the contents of their bucket matches with the contents of your bucket the less friction you will experience down the road. The closer the match also means less cups are likely to come out of each others bucket. The first thing we need is to know who we are and the last thing we need is for someone else to always be challenging who we are and taking cups from our bucket. Amen!

HOW CAN I KNOW FOR SURE I WILL NOT PICK THE WRONG PERSON AGAIN?

You have already experienced being in a bad relationship and there is no way you want to do that again. You may likely feel broken and are still gradually restoring your health and strength. Companionship is important to you but you are afraid of walking right back into something bad like you had before.

The problem is that there are no guarantees. However, there are simple steps that you can take to cover as many bases as possible. Let us consider the basics.

**Start with
healthy dating**

First, make sure you are as healthy as you can be. Build your bucket. Take time for yourself. Heal up. Know who you are.

Second, select someone who is healthy. Select an individual, who has a bucket, knows who they are and is strong.

After the basics, begin navigating your relationship. Start with healthy dating, which involves doing hours and hours and hours of talking. Get to know your date and pay attention to whether or not they are getting to know you.

Often couples when they start dating become sexually involved quite early in the relationship. It is not for me to decide at what point you become sexually involved in a relationship. The point is that there needs to be enough talking to each other in order to really <u>know</u> a person.

Flags. Red flags and yellow flags often come up during the period of dating, and you can pay attention to these flags. A flag is a metaphor for an issue or concern you have about the relationship or the other person. Don't ignore the flags! Immediately address the flag with your partner or spouse as they arise.

If the issues are not resolved and a cup comes out of your bucket again and again, then you are not with the right person. You will clearly know that you are with the wrong person. There needs to be complete respect from both individuals in order for the relationship to work. Remember – it is important to me to be respected.

CHAPTER V
CONCLUSION

HOW CAN YOU BECOME
A STRONGER THINKER?

You may start noticing some of your friends are great thinkers and respond to life from a **thinking** orientation. You see yourself operating from more of **feeling** orientation and wished you could be more like them. Some of you reading this see yourself as primarily a doing person.

I think the thinkers have it made and are in the best position to deal with the tough situations in life. I also think that all of us can become better thinkers. After we build our bucket then we must become more self-aware. It is a wonderful ability to be so aware of how we think, feel and do.

Once our self-awareness grows, we can begin employing the skills necessary to become a highly efficient thinker.

It is ok to be a **feeling** person and a **doing** person, but it is important to be a good **thinker**. To have each of these three qualities **equally** would help each of us not to struggle so much, make better choices and to become happier in life.

    Practice makes perfect applies to a great golfer. Practicing your good thinking also will make you a good thinker. Athletes call it muscle memory.

    What is it you are to think upon? Look to your bucket and all the wonderful things it holds.

FOLLOW – UP

If you would like further assistance to apply this material or to make improvement in other areas of your life, please contact Valerie direct.

Valerie J. Friesen provides Personal Improvement Coaching and Counselling Services from her office or over the telephone. To arrange for your private session, please contact Valerie the following method.

Contact   Valerie J. Friesen
            203 10090 152nd Street
            Surrey, BC, Canada
            V3R 8X8

            604-589-5560

ISBN 1412090186-0

Edwards Brothers Malloy
Thorofare, NJ USA
May 2, 2014